10 Steps for Dealing with Toxic People

with Toxic People

Louis Yandoli

DEDICATION

To my wife, cherished family, my steadfast friends, and all those who have ignited the flame of inspiration along my journey:

This book is a testament to the love, support, and encouragement you all generously offered. Your belief in me has been the bedrock upon which these pages have come to life.

In gratitude and admiration, I dedicate this work to each of you. May it symbolize our shared journey and remind us that we can conquer the highest peaks together. Thank you.

CONTENTS

ABOUT THE AUTHOR

Louis Yandoli is a distinguished professional with over two decades of experience in various consulting and management roles within Global Fortune 500 companies. He holds a bachelor's degree in chemical engineering from Lehigh University and began his career at ExxonMobil, where he was immediately assigned to an international post in Singapore. After a successful four-year stint, particularly in collaborating with clients in Japan, Louis returned to the United States. He pursued a master's degree in engineering, attending classes during evenings and weekends while continuing to work.

In 2013, Louis was awarded a full scholarship to attend Hitotsubashi University in Tokyo, Japan, where he completed his MBA in just one year and graduated at the top of his class. Upon returning to the United States, he transitioned his career to cybersecurity, joining Sony as a Cyber Security Professional.

Louis is passionate about many hobbies, such as cooking, investing, maintaining a healthy lifestyle, acquiring new skills, raising his two young children, and appreciating fine food and wine.

The concept of his "10 Step" series was born out of a conversation with a close friend about sharing knowledge and experiences with others facing similar challenges. Louis hopes that his insights, examples, and wisdom will empower readers to achieve their goals, whatever they may be.

THE 10-STEP APPROACH EXPLAINED

The "10 Steps to Success" book series offers a comprehensive yet easily digestible approach to mastering various skills and topics. Each book in the series follows the same structured format, guiding readers through ten carefully designed steps that build upon one another to create a holistic understanding of the subject matter. This section will explore the standard approach used throughout the "10 Steps to Success" series and explain how this book adheres to the same principles.

1. Embracing the 10-Step Approach

Each "10 Steps to Success" book begins by breaking down a complex subject into ten manageable steps. These steps are designed to be informative and practical, offering readers insights, techniques, and actionable tips they can apply to their lives or work. Focusing on one step at a time allows readers to process and retain the information presented more efficiently, leading to a more effective learning experience.

2. Understanding the Connections Between Steps

While each step in the "10 Steps to Success" series can be valuable on its own, the true power of the approach lies in the connections between the steps. As readers progress through the book, they will find that each step builds upon the previous one, weaving together a cohesive narrative that reinforces key concepts and deepens understanding. By following the steps in sequence, readers can develop a comprehensive and well-rounded mastery of the subject.

3. Efficient and Bite-Sized Learning

The "10 Steps to Success" approach maximizes efficiency by delivering knowledge and information in bite-sized chunks.

Each step is focused and concise, allowing readers to quickly grasp and apply the core concepts in their own lives. This modular format also makes it easy for readers to refer back to specific steps as needed, reinforcing their learning and ensuring they have the tools they need to succeed.

4. Completing the Journey

By working through all ten steps in the "10 Steps to Success" series, readers will thoroughly understand the subject matter and gain the knowledge and skills necessary to succeed in their chosen field or endeavor. In addition, the series provides a clear roadmap for success, guiding readers step by step through the learning process and empowering them to take control of their personal and professional growth.

In summary, the "10 Steps to Success" approach is a proven and effective method for mastering complex subjects and developing new skills. By breaking down topics into manageable steps, connecting the dots between each step, and delivering information in an efficient and digestible format, the series enables readers to deeply understand the subject matter and apply their newfound knowledge to succeed. So, as you embark on your 10-step journey, remember to take your time, trust the process, and enjoy the rewards of mastering a new skill or subject.

5. Personal Experience and Tested Techniques

One of the key strengths of the "10 Steps to Success" series is that the guidance, techniques, and processes presented in each book are not theoretical concepts created in a vacuum. Instead, they are grounded in my personal and professional experiences, accumulated over 20 years of trial and error, learning from mistakes, and refining strategies to optimize outcomes.

Throughout the series, I share my insights and lessons learned from my own experience, offering practical examples and case studies that demonstrate how the 10-step approach has been successfully applied in real-life situations. Then, drawing on these experiences, I hope to provide a relatable and authentic perspective on the subject matter, making it more accessible and engaging for readers.

Moreover, my extensive background in various consulting and management positions across Global Fortune 500 companies has provided a wealth of knowledge and expertise that has been distilled into the "10 Steps to Success" series. This ensures that the advice and techniques offered in each book are relevant, applicable, tested, and proven to deliver results.

As you work through the 10 steps in this book, you can take comfort in knowing that the guidance you are receiving has been honed and refined through years of real-world experience. This practical foundation will help you better understand the concepts and techniques presented and equip you with the confidence and tools necessary to apply them effectively in your professional or personal pursuits.

HELPFUL RESOURCES AND REFERENCES

In this section, I have compiled a selection of books and resources that have greatly influenced and inspired the content of this book. These references, written by experts in the field, provide valuable insights, tips, and techniques that can further enhance your understanding and skills. Each has helped me immensely in my decades of personal and professional experience thinking through these 10 steps.

Exploring these resources will deepen your knowledge and help you discover additional strategies and ideas to take your learning to the next level. Whether you seek more detailed guidance, practical examples, or inspiration from the best in the business, this curated list of resources is an excellent starting point for your continued learning growth.

1. "Emotional Blackmail: When the People in Your Life Use Fear, Obligation, and Guilt to Manipulate You" by Susan Forward, 1997, Harpercollins.
   - Offers insights into how emotional blackmail can turn into a destructive cycle and how to break free from it.

2. "Toxic People: Dealing With Dysfunctional Relationships" by Tim Cantopher, 2017, Sheldon Press.
   - Provides strategies for recognizing and dealing with people who take joy in creating chaos.

3. "In Sheep's Clothing: Understanding and Dealing with Manipulative People" by George K. Simon, 1996, A.J. Christopher & Co.

- Explains how to recognize manipulative people, understand their tactics, and respond effectively.

4. "Who's Pulling Your Strings? How to Break the Cycle of Manipulation" by Harriet Braiker, 2004, McGraw-Hill Education.
    - Presents strategies to stop manipulation, regain control, and maintain personal boundaries.

5. "The Gaslight Effect: How to Spot and Survive the Hidden Manipulation Others Use to Control Your Life" by Dr. Robin Stern, 2007, Harmony.
    - Offers a guide to recognizing, understanding, and managing the phenomenon of gaslighting.

6. "Dealing with People You Can't Stand, Revised and Expanded Third Edition: How to Bring Out the Best in People at Their Worst" by Dr. Rick Brinkman & Dr. Rick Kirschner, 2012, McGraw-Hill Education.
    - Shares strategies for handling difficult people and conflict in the workplace.

7. "Nasty People" by Jay Carter, 2003, McGraw-Hill Education.
    - Provides insights into why people act negatively and how to respond effectively.

8. "The No Asshole Rule: Building a Civilized Workplace and Surviving One That Isn't" by Robert I. Sutton, 2007, Grand Central Publishing.
    - Discusses how toxic individuals can damage workplace culture and provides practical tips for creating a more positive environment.

9. "Emotional Vampires: Dealing With People Who Drain You Dry" by Albert J. Bernstein, 2000, McGraw-Hill Education.
   - Illustrates how to protect oneself from individuals who suck the emotional energy out of us.

10. "Toxic Parents: Overcoming Their Hurtful Legacy and Reclaiming Your Life" by Susan Forward, 2002, Bantam.
    - Explores the complex dynamics of toxic parent-child relationships and offers a path toward healing.

11. "The Narcissist Next Door: Understanding the Monster in Your Family, in Your Office, in Your Bed-in Your World" by Jeffrey Kluger, 2014, Riverhead Books.
    - Helps in understanding and dealing with narcissists in personal and professional life.

12. "The Sociopath Next Door" by Martha Stout, 2005, Harmony.
    - Explores the world of sociopaths and provides strategies for recognizing and dealing with them.

13. "Boundaries: When to Say Yes, How to Say No To Take Control of Your Life" by Dr. Henry Cloud & Dr. John Townsend, 1992, Zondervan.
    - Teaches how to establish personal boundaries to improve one's relationships and mental health.

14. "Stop Walking on Eggshells: Taking Your Life Back When Someone You Care About Has Borderline

Personality Disorder" by Paul T. Mason & Randi Kreger, 1998, New Harbinger Publications.
- Gives practical advice for those dealing with a loved one with borderline personality disorder.

15. "Healing from Hidden Abuse: A Journey Through the Stages of Recovery from Psychological Abuse" by Shannon Thomas, 2016, MAST Publishing House.
- Unfolds the path of healing from psychological abuse by toxic people.

16. "Why Does He Do That?: Inside the Minds of Angry and Controlling Men" by Lundy Bancroft, 2002, Berkley Books.
- Examines the mindset of abusive men and provides guidance for dealing with such individuals.

17. "When the Body Says No: The Cost of Hidden Stress" by Gabor Maté, 2003, Knopf Canada.
- Explains how chronic stress can lead to serious physical illnesses, especially from dealing with toxic people.

18. "It's All Your Fault!: 12 Tips for Managing People Who Blame Others for Everything" by Bill Eddy, 2011, Unhooked Books.
- Provides techniques for dealing with people who shift blame onto others.

19. "Controlling People: How to Recognize, Understand, and Deal with People Who Try to Control You" by Patricia Evans, 2002, Adams Media.
- Discusses how to recognize and handle people who are controlling.

20. "Disarming the Narcissist: Surviving and Thriving with the Self-Absorbed" by Wendy T. Behary, 2008, New Harbinger Publications.
    - Offers effective strategies for dealing effectively with someone narcissistic.

INTRODUCTION

Welcome to a journey of awareness, understanding, and transformation. These ten steps will guide you through the labyrinth of toxic relationships, equipping you with the tools and insights necessary to recognize, manage, and rise above toxic interactions.

The focus of this book is rooted in the uncomfortable reality that toxic people are an unfortunate and all too familiar part of life. Toxic individuals, whether colleagues, family members, friends, or even intimate partners, can drain our energy, undermine our self-esteem, and create conflict and chaos in our lives.

However, within these pages, we will not only learn how to deal with these individuals but also how to turn adversity into strength, transform chaos into order, and ultimately, how to thrive amidst and beyond toxicity.

Understanding Toxicity

The concept of toxicity can be nebulous, often misused or misunderstood. However, in the context of relationships, a toxic individual is one whose behavior consistently brings negative energy and discord, often at the expense of other people's well-being and peace.

This toxicity can manifest in various forms – from constant criticism, passive-aggressive behavior, manipulation, and narcissism to more overt actions such as emotional, verbal, or even physical abuse. While these behaviors may be more visible in some individuals than in others, their impact can be profound and damaging, leaving lasting scars that can take time and considerable effort to heal.

The Importance of the Journey

You may ask why we must delve into this somber subject. The reason is simple, yet profound – knowledge is power. Understanding toxic behavior allows us to recognize it, respond to it appropriately, and protect our mental and emotional well-being. It equips us with the tools to navigate toxic relationships effectively and reduce potential harm.

Furthermore, this process is not merely about surviving toxic relationships but learning and growing from these experiences. It is about reclaiming our power, rediscovering our self-worth, and cultivating resilience and emotional intelligence. It is about turning adversity into a stepping-stone for personal growth and self-improvement.

Overview of the Steps Ahead

This book is structured into ten steps, each exploring different facets of dealing with toxic individuals and providing practical strategies and insights. We start with self-awareness, understanding our emotions and reactions, before moving onto recognizing toxic behaviors in others. We then delve into establishing boundaries and cultivating emotional intelligence, both crucial tools in managing toxic relationships.

Later on, we discuss the value of support systems, the importance of self-care, and the role of assertive communication in dealing with toxic people. We explore specific strategies for handling toxic individuals in various contexts, such as the workplace, within families, and in social settings.

We conclude on personal growth from these experiences, understanding when it is time to move on from a toxic relationship, and how to do so in a healthy, respectful manner. The design of this book is not just to be read but to be used. It is a tool, a guide, and a companion on your steps toward healthier and more fulfilling relationships.

You Are Not Alone

Finally, it is essential to remember that you are not alone in this journey. Countless others have walked and are walking this path. The experiences shared and the strategies suggested within these pages have been gathered from a wealth of sources, including expert psychologists, therapists, and individuals who have faced and overcome toxic relationships in their lives.

In the following steps, I invite you to engage, question, reflect, and most importantly, apply what resonates with you to your life. Take the time to absorb the information, ponder the insights, and practice the strategies.

Remember, this is not a sprint but a marathon. It involves introspection, patience, and perseverance. At times, the road may be a bit difficult, even painful, but know that every step you take, no matter how small, is a step towards a healthier, happier you.

Now, let us embark together toward understanding, growth, and transformation. Let us embrace an approach that will equip us with the knowledge, tools, and resilience to deal with toxic people, grow from these experiences, and ultimately thrive. Thank you for being here and choosing to take this path. Let us begin.

1 RECOGNIZING TOXIC PEOPLE

Recognizing toxic people is the first critical step towards protecting yourself and maintaining your mental well-being. Toxic people are individuals who consistently exhibit behaviors that can be harmful to others, often resulting in the erosion of peace and harmony in relationships. These behaviors may include manipulation, persistent negativity, lack of empathy, or an overbearing need for control.

This step will delve into the common characteristics of toxic individuals and discuss the different forms toxicity can take. It is important to remember, however, that we are all capable of toxic behaviors at times - the key differentiator is the persistent pattern of these behaviors that is disruptive to the well-being of others.

Manipulative Behavior

One of the most common traits of toxic people is their use of manipulation to control others. Manipulative individuals are often very subtle in their tactics, making it difficult for their victims to realize they are being manipulated. They may use emotional blackmail, guilt, or even feign helplessness to get what they want.

A manipulative person might consistently make you feel guilty for not spending time with them, even when you have other important commitments. Or they might regularly ask for favors but rarely return them, using excuses or emotional appeals to get out of reciprocal responsibility.

Persistent Negativity

Toxic people often have a pervasive negative outlook on life. They may frequently complain, criticize, or see the worst in every situation. This consistent negativity can be draining for those around them, causing a generally cheerful atmosphere to turn sour. They might be the ones who are always finding faults, complaining about others, or creating dramas out of minor inconveniences.

However, it is essential to distinguish between someone going through a difficult time and expressing their emotions versus a consistently negative person. Everyone has bad days and may vent or express negative emotions - the key difference is the persistence and extent of the negativity.

Lack of Empathy

Empathy, the ability to understand and share the feelings of others, is often lacking in toxic individuals. As a result, they may disregard others' feelings, dismiss their problems, or fail to show any genuine concern for others' emotional well-being. Lack of empathy can result in one-sided relationships where the toxic person's needs and feelings are prioritized above all else.

An individual lacking empathy might brush off your concerns or problems as trivial or insist that their issues are always much worse. They might consistently turn the conversation back to themselves, showing little to no interest in your experiences or feelings.

Overbearing Need for Control

Toxic people often exhibit an intense need to control others and their environment. This control can take many forms, from overt demands to subtle manipulation. These individuals might have rigid expectations and become upset when things do not go exactly their way.

A controlling person might try to dictate how you spend your time, who you spend it with, or how you behave. They might become angry or distressed if they feel they are not in control, leading to conflict and unease.

It is important to remember that these behaviors are not always clear-cut, and a toxic person may not exhibit all these traits. The critical aspect is the consistent pattern of these behaviors and their impact on those around them. Recognizing these signs is the first step towards dealing with toxic people effectively.

Excessive Criticism

Another common trait of toxic individuals is their tendency to excessively criticize others. While constructive criticism is a healthy and necessary part of any relationship, toxic people often use criticism to belittle, control, and undermine the confidence of those around them. Moreover, this type of criticism is usually unjust, unasked for, and delivered in a way that is hurtful rather than helpful.

A toxic person might constantly find faults in your work, criticize your personal choices, or attack your character traits. The continuous barrage of critique can chip away at your self-esteem, leading to self-doubt and diminished confidence.

Victim Mentality

Toxic people often employ a victim mentality as a way to manipulate and control others. They tend to deflect responsibility for their actions, blaming others or external circumstances for their behavior or failures. They might frequently lament about their life, emphasizing how they are always the victim, and fail to take responsibility for their actions.

A person exhibiting a victim mentality might always blame their colleagues for their poor work performance, their friends for their social problems, or their family for their personal issues. They rarely admit to their mistakes or take steps to improve their situation, preferring instead to remain in their victim role and avoid taking responsibility.

Respect for Boundaries

One common trait among toxic people is their disregard for personal boundaries. As a result, they may frequently overstep or ignore your boundaries, causing you to feel uncomfortable or violated. This disregard can apply to physical boundaries, such as personal space or belongings, and psychological boundaries, like your time, emotions, or personal experiences.

A toxic person might continuously borrow your things without asking, demand your time regardless of your commitments, or insist on discussing topics you are uncomfortable with. They show little respect for your personal space, needs, or feelings, leading to one-sided relationships where your boundaries are consistently violated.

Passive-Aggressive Behavior

Toxic people often resort to passive-aggressive behaviors when expressing discontent or disagreement. Instead of addressing issues openly and honestly, they might opt for indirect communication like subtle insults, sarcastic remarks, or sullen behavior intended to express their displeasure.

A passive-aggressive individual might give you the silent treatment when they are upset with you, make sarcastic remarks about your work, or use subtle put-downs disguised as jokes. This indirect form of hostility can create a stressful environment, making interactions tense and unpleasant.

Recognizing toxic individuals' traits can help you identify potentially harmful relationships and take steps to protect yourself. However, remember that people can change;

occasional lapses in these behaviors do not necessarily label someone as 'toxic.' Consistency and frequency are key – it is the persistent, long-term pattern of these behaviors that cause distress and harm to others, which ultimately characterizes a person as toxic.

In the following steps, we will delve into how you can effectively handle and protect yourself from the damaging impact of toxic individuals. The recognition of these traits forms the foundation upon which these future strategies are built. By understanding these common characteristics and behaviors, you have taken the first crucial step toward dealing with toxic individuals in your life.

2 UNDERSTANDING YOUR ROLE

In the dance of toxicity, it takes two to tango. While it is easier to point fingers and label another as toxic, it is crucial to reflect upon our own behaviors, attitudes, and patterns that might enable or attract such individuals. After recognizing toxic individuals, the next step involves introspection - understanding your role in the dynamic.

Are You a People-Pleaser?

People-pleasers often find themselves the target of toxic individuals. They are usually kind-hearted, generous, and eager to keep harmony, even at their own expense. Toxic individuals may exploit these traits, knowing that a people-pleaser will go to great lengths to avoid conflict and maintain peace.

However, it is essential to acknowledge that being nice isn't the issue – it's the lack of boundaries and the inability to say 'no' when necessary that can attract toxicity. Examine your own patterns: do you often agree to things you are uncomfortable with just to avoid conflict? Do you feel guilty when you prioritize your needs? Answering such questions can shed light on whether you tend to people-please, thus inadvertently attracting toxic people.

Unresolved Personal Issues

Unresolved personal issues can also make us susceptible to toxic relationships. These issues might stem from past traumas, low self-esteem, or previous toxic relationships, leading us to accept behaviors we otherwise would not. A deep-seated belief of being 'unworthy' of love and respect, for instance, might lead us to accept less than we deserve.

The healing process begins with acknowledging these personal issues and seeking help if necessary. This could involve therapy, self-help books, or supportive communities, where one can learn healthier relationship patterns and rebuild their self-esteem.

The Savior Complex

Some people are naturally inclined towards helping others – to the point where they feel responsible for 'saving' or 'fixing' them. This 'savior complex' can lead us into toxic relationships, as we might get drawn to individuals exhibiting problematic behaviors, believing we can change them for the better.

But it is essential to understand that lasting change comes from within. We cannot force someone to change if they are not willing or ready. It is not your responsibility to fix others, especially at the expense of your own well-being. Recognizing if you harbor a savior complex can help prevent you from getting into unhealthy dynamics.

Establishing and Enforcing Boundaries

One of the significant roles we play in our relationships is establishing and enforcing our boundaries. If we often let others cross our boundaries without consequences, we signal to them that such behavior is acceptable.

Consider your past relationships and interactions: Have you made your boundaries clear? What happens when someone crosses them? Do you enforce consequences, or do you let it slide? Reflecting on these can help you understand your role in allowing toxic behaviors.

The purpose of this self-reflection is not to blame yourself but to empower you. By understanding your role, you can take steps to change the dynamics, establish healthier boundaries, and prevent yourself from falling into similar patterns in the future. Remember, it is not about fault but about responsibility and growth.

The Role of Self-Esteem

Self-esteem plays a vital role in the type of relationships we develop. Those with low self-esteem often undervalue themselves and may tolerate toxic behaviors as a result. They might struggle to assert themselves, express their needs, or believe they deserve respect in their relationships.

A healthy level of self-esteem is the belief in one is worth. When we value ourselves, we are less likely to tolerate mistreatment or disrespect. Instead, we seek relationships that honor our worth and positively reflect our self-esteem.

Reflect on your self-esteem: How do you view yourself? Do you believe you deserve respect, kindness, and understanding in your relationships? If you often doubt your worth, it might be time to focus on building your self-esteem. This could involve therapy, self-care practices, or even self-help resources that foster a healthier self-image.

Communication Style

Our communication style can also play a role in how we interact with toxic individuals. Passive communicators, for instance, may struggle to express their needs or feelings effectively, making them a target for manipulative individuals.

On the other hand, aggressive communicators might escalate conflicts, fueling the toxic dynamic. The ideal communication style is assertive – expressing your needs and feelings respectfully and honestly without infringing on others' rights.

Consider your own communication style: Are you passive, often agreeing to avoid conflict? Or perhaps you are aggressive, expressing your needs without considering others'? Or maybe you are passive-aggressive, showing your displeasure indirectly? Recognizing your communication style can help you understand your role in toxic dynamics.

Patterns from the Past

Our past can significantly influence our present. We might have learned unhealthy relationship patterns from our parents or previous relationships. These patterns can be deeply ingrained, leading us to repeat them in our current relationships, often without realizing it.

Reflecting on your past can help you identify these patterns. Did your parents have a healthy relationship? What kind of relationships did they model for you? Did you have past relationships that were toxic? How did you handle them? Unpacking these experiences can provide valuable insights into your current behaviors and tendencies.

Breaking the Cycle

Understanding your role is about recognizing that you have the power to break the cycle of toxicity. By acknowledging your behaviors and attitudes that might be enabling toxicity, you are taking the first step toward change. You are saying, "I have a role in this, and I can change it."

You might need to learn new skills, such as assertive communication or setting boundaries. You might need to work on personal issues, like boosting your self-esteem or resolving past traumas. Or you might need to let go of the belief that you can save or change others.

The journey might be challenging, but it is also empowering. Every step you take towards understanding your role is a step towards healthier relationships, stronger self-esteem, and a happier life.

3   ESTABLISHING BOUNDARIES

Understanding your role in the toxicity dance is crucial, but it is just the beginning. The next step in dealing with toxic people involves setting firm, clear boundaries. As mentioned briefly in the previous step, boundaries serve as guidelines for acceptable behavior from others. They reflect your self-respect and ensure that your needs and feelings are respected.

Defining Personal Boundaries

Personal boundaries are a reflection of your needs, values, and limits. They vary from person to person, as everyone has unique needs and comfort levels. Some might feel comfortable with close physical proximity, while others might need more personal space. Some people might be open to discussing their personal life, while others might prefer to keep such matters private.

Defining your boundaries involves self-reflection and understanding your needs and values. Reflect on your past experiences - when did you feel uncomfortable, disrespected, or violated? These instances often signal crossed boundaries and can guide you in establishing your own.

Communicating Your Boundaries

Once you have defined your boundaries, the next step is to communicate them effectively. It might feel uncomfortable, especially if you are not used to asserting yourself, but it is crucial to express your boundaries clearly and assertively.

Be direct about what you are comfortable with and what you are not. Use "I" statements to express your feelings without blaming or criticizing the other person. For example, instead of saying, "You're always crossing the line," you might say, "I feel uncomfortable when you comment on my personal life."

The Right to Set Boundaries

People often struggle with setting boundaries, fearing they might come off as rude or selfish. However, it is essential to recognize that you have a right to set boundaries. It does not make you a bad person - in fact, it signifies respect for yourself and others.

Everyone has their own comfort levels and limits, and it is completely okay to express them. If someone reacts negatively to your boundaries, it is a reflection of them, not you. You are not responsible for their reactions or emotions - your first responsibility is toward your well-being.

Boundaries in Different Contexts

Different relationships might require different boundaries. For instance, the boundaries you set with a colleague might be different from those you set with a friend or a family member. Moreover, different situations might also call for different boundaries.

For example, in a professional setting, you might set boundaries around your working hours or your responsibilities. In a personal relationship, you might set boundaries around personal space, communication style, or how you spend your time together. It is essential to consider the context and adjust your boundaries accordingly.

Enforcing Your Boundaries

Establishing boundaries is not enough - you also need to enforce them. If someone crosses your boundaries, it is crucial to address it immediately and assertively. Let them know that their behavior is unacceptable and that you expect respect for your boundaries.

Enforcing boundaries might involve expressing your discomfort, requesting a change in behavior, or, in some cases, distancing yourself from the person. Remember, you do not have to justify, argue, defend, or negotiate your boundaries. They are non-negotiable and must be respected.

Dealing with Boundary Violations

Despite clear communication and enforcement, some people might repeatedly violate your boundaries. These violations can range from subtle (e.g., dismissive remarks or passive aggression) to more overt (e.g., manipulation or disrespect). Dealing with such violations involves standing firm on your boundaries and possibly reconsidering your relationship with the violator.

For repeated violations, you might need to escalate your response. This could mean limiting contact with the person, seeking mediation, or, in extreme cases, ending the relationship. It is essential to prioritize your well-being and not allow guilt or fear to keep you in a toxic dynamic.

The Role of Self-Care in Setting Boundaries

Setting boundaries also ties into self-care. When we care for ourselves, we recognize our worth and are less likely to tolerate disrespect or mistreatment. Self-care is not just about bubble baths and spa days - it is about attending to your physical, emotional, mental, and spiritual needs.

Self-care might involve getting enough rest, eating healthily, exercising, seeking therapy, practicing mindfulness, or spending time on hobbies. It also means saying 'no' when you are overwhelmed, taking breaks when needed, and seeking help when you are struggling.

Self-care fosters self-respect and self-love, making it easier for us to establish and enforce boundaries. By taking care of ourselves, we signal to others that we value our well-being and expect others to do the same.

Respecting Others' Boundaries

Just as we expect others to respect our boundaries, we should respect theirs as well. It involves acknowledging their boundaries and adhering to them, even if they are different from ours. It is essential for creating respectful, healthy relationships.

Respecting boundaries might involve understanding their comfort levels, respecting their personal space, or honoring their needs and feelings. If you are unsure about someone's boundaries, it is always better to ask than assume.

In the end, setting boundaries is about honoring your worth and fostering mutual respect in your relationships. It is not always easy, but it is necessary for dealing with toxic people and cultivating healthier dynamics. As you learn to set and enforce boundaries, you are likely to experience a significant shift in your relationships - less toxicity and more respect, understanding, and overall health.

The Importance of Consistency

One of the key aspects of setting and enforcing boundaries is consistency. Inconsistent boundaries can lead to confusion and misunderstanding. It is crucial to maintain a consistent stance on your boundaries to ensure they are respected.

Consistency does not mean inflexibility. Your boundaries may change over time, and that is completely acceptable. However, changes should be communicated clearly and upheld consistently. For example, if you have decided to stop working on weekends, stick to this boundary consistently, barring exceptional circumstances.

Boundaries and Mental Health

Boundaries are essential not just for healthy relationships but also for mental health. Disrespect or violation of boundaries can lead to feelings of disrespect, violation, stress, anxiety, or even trauma. By setting boundaries, you can protect your mental health and well-being.

If you are finding it challenging to set or enforce boundaries, you might find it helpful to seek professional help. A therapist can provide valuable insights into your boundary issues and equip you with the skills to handle them more effectively.

Personal Growth and Boundaries

Setting boundaries can lead to personal growth. It encourages self-awareness as you reflect on your needs, values, and comfort levels. It fosters assertiveness as you communicate and enforce your boundaries. It also boosts self-esteem and self-respect as you honor your worth.

Furthermore, setting boundaries can transform your relationships. You are likely to experience less toxicity and more respect, understanding, and healthy interactions. As a result, you might find yourself feeling more confident, valued, and empowered.

Final Thoughts on Setting Boundaries

In conclusion, setting boundaries is a critical step in dealing with toxic people. It is about recognizing your worth, expressing your needs, and ensuring that they are respected. It might be challenging, especially if you are not used to asserting yourself or if you are dealing with particularly toxic individuals. But it is a journey worth undertaking.

By setting boundaries, you are not only protecting your well-being but also fostering healthier, more respectful relationships. You are empowering yourself to step out of toxic dynamics and step into healthier, more fulfilling interactions.

4   A SUPPORT NETWORK

Dealing with toxic people can be mentally and emotionally draining. Having a supportive network around you can make this process much more manageable. This network can comprise friends, family members, mentors, therapists, or anyone who understands your situation and offers unconditional support.

The Role of a Supportive Network

When you are dealing with toxic people, you might often find yourself feeling isolated, misunderstood, or overwhelmed. A supportive network can provide comfort, validation, and guidance during such times.

Having people who validate your feelings and experiences can be incredibly healing. It can reassure you that you are not alone or misunderstood. It can affirm that your feelings and reactions are valid and that it is okay to stand up for yourself.

Supportive individuals can also provide guidance and advice. They can offer a fresh perspective on your situation, suggest potential coping strategies, or share their own experiences. They can help you navigate through the complexities of dealing with toxic people and provide emotional support when you are feeling low.

Building a Supportive Network

If you do not already have a supportive network, it is never too late to start building one. It can begin with reaching out to people you trust and feel comfortable with. It could be a close friend, a family member, a mentor, or a counselor.

It is essential to choose people who understand your situation and offer non-judgmental support. They should respect your boundaries, validate your feelings, and support your decisions. It is equally important that these relationships are reciprocal - that you also offer support and understanding to them.

Engaging in social activities can also help you build a supportive network. This could involve joining clubs, participating in community events, volunteering, or taking up a new hobby. These activities can help you meet like-minded individuals and form meaningful connections.

Online communities can also be a valuable source of support. Numerous forums, groups, and platforms cater to people dealing with toxic individuals. They can offer a space to share your experiences, seek advice, or simply find solace in knowing that others are going through similar experiences.

Maintaining a Supportive Network

Building a supportive network is just the first step; maintaining it is equally important. This can involve regular communication, mutual support, and respect for each other's boundaries.

Regular communication keeps the connection alive. It can involve sharing updates, discussing challenges, or simply catching up. It is important to ensure that the communication is two-way - both parties should feel heard and valued.

Mutual support is another crucial aspect. While it is important to seek support from others, offering your support to them is equally vital. It is about being there for each other, offering comfort and assistance in times of need.

Respecting each other's boundaries is also key. This can involve understanding their comfort levels, respecting their personal space, and honoring their needs and feelings. Just as we expect others to respect our boundaries, we should respect theirs too.

The Importance of Professional Help

While friends, family, and peers can provide valuable support, professional help can also be crucial. Professionals like psychologists, therapists, or counselors can provide a safe, confidential space to explore your feelings and challenges.

Professional help can also provide you with effective coping strategies, resources, and tools to deal with toxic people. They can offer a fresh, unbiased perspective on your situation and help you navigate through it more effectively.

Building Internal Support Systems

Apart from external support, building internal support systems is also crucial. This can involve self-care practices, self-validation, and self-compassion.

Self-care practices like regular exercise, healthy eating, adequate sleep, mindfulness, or hobbies can boost your mental and emotional health. They can help you manage stress, enhance your mood, and increase your resilience.

Self-validation involves acknowledging your feelings and experiences, affirming that they are valid and important. It is about listening to your inner voice and trusting your instincts.

Self-compassion involves being kind and understanding toward yourself, especially during challenging times. It is about acknowledging your struggles, accepting your imperfections, and treating yourself with the same kindness and understanding that you would treat a friend.

Nurturing a supportive network is a critical step in dealing with toxic people. It involves building and maintaining supportive relationships, seeking professional help, and fostering internal support systems. By surrounding yourself with positive influences and reinforcing your inner strength, you can navigate through the challenges of dealing with toxic people more effectively.

How Support Networks Serve as a Resource

A supportive network is not just a comfort; it can also be a valuable resource. Those in your network can provide advice, share their own experiences, offer new perspectives, and help you brainstorm solutions to challenges you are facing with toxic people.

The combined experiences of your network may also bring to light patterns of behavior that you had not recognized. They can provide insight into how others have successfully navigated similar situations and what you might expect moving forward. Their input can help you prepare for potential challenges and arm you with strategies to manage them effectively.

Empathy and Understanding

A primary benefit of a supportive network is the empathy and understanding it provides. Often, toxic people can make you feel isolated and misunderstood. Having people who genuinely understand and empathize with your situation can be incredibly healing. It can help you realize that you are not alone, that your feelings are valid, and that it is okay to seek help.

Building Resilience

A supportive network can also play a crucial role in building your resilience. The emotional support and guidance they provide can boost your confidence and coping skills, making you more resilient to the challenges posed by toxic people.

Furthermore, your network can help you focus on your strengths and potential, rather than the negative elements in your life. This can foster a sense of self-efficacy and empowerment, reinforcing your resilience against the toxic influences in your life.

Looking Ahead

Building and maintaining a supportive network is a continuous process. It requires effort, understanding, and mutual respect. However, the benefits it offers make it worth the effort.

Fostering a supportive network is not about dependency but about interdependency - a mutual, reciprocal relationship where everyone involved gives and receives support. It fosters a sense of belonging and community, reinforcing the belief that others are with you on your journey. Your supportive network is an invaluable step when dealing with toxic people. The comfort, guidance, and strength it offers can help you navigate the challenges more effectively and foster healthier dynamics in your life.

Remember, you are not alone. There are people who understand, care, and want to help. By seeking and accepting their support, you are not only empowering yourself but also fostering a community of understanding, empathy, and mutual support. This marks the end of Step 4, an important stage in your journey toward dealing with toxic individuals. We will continue to explore further steps, each contributing to your overall strategy and resilience in the face of toxicity.

5 MINDFULNESS AND SELF-CARE

In the battle against toxicity, it is easy to lose sight of one crucial fact - the importance of looking after oneself. Engaging with toxic people can be mentally, emotionally, and sometimes even physically draining. This makes practicing mindfulness and self-care an essential part of dealing with toxic people.

Mindfulness

Mindfulness refers to the practice of being fully present and engaged in the current moment. It involves paying attention to your thoughts, feelings, and physical sensations without judgment. This can be particularly helpful in situations involving toxic individuals.

For example, mindfulness can help you become more aware of your emotions and reactions during interactions with toxic people. You might notice feelings of stress, anxiety, anger, or sadness. By being mindful, you can recognize these emotions as they arise, giving you the opportunity to manage them more effectively.

Mindfulness also promotes self-awareness. It can help you recognize patterns in your interactions with toxic individuals and gain insights into how they affect you. This increased self-awareness can then guide you in establishing boundaries, seeking support, or taking other steps to protect your well-being.

There are various ways to practice mindfulness. These include mindfulness meditation, yoga, mindful eating, or simply taking a few moments each day to check in with yourself and your feelings.

Self-Care

Self-care involves activities and practices that you engage in to relax, replenish your energy, and take care of your physical, emotional, and mental health. It is about treating yourself with kindness and understanding, recognizing your needs, and taking the time to meet them.

Self-care is not an act of indulgence or selfishness, as some might believe. Instead, it is a necessary part of maintaining your well-being, especially when dealing with toxic people. Just like you cannot pour from an empty cup, you cannot effectively deal with toxicity if you are not taking care of yourself.

Mindfulness in Everyday Life

Implementing mindfulness in your daily life can be as simple as taking a few moments each day to focus on your breath, taking a mindful walk, or practicing mindfulness during routine tasks like washing dishes or brushing your teeth. It is about being present and fully engaged in whatever you are doing rather than letting your mind wander or getting caught up in stress or worries.

Mindful journaling is another great way to practice mindfulness. It allows you to explore your thoughts and feelings in a non-judgmental way. You could write about your interactions with toxic people, your reactions, your feelings, or anything else that comes to mind. This can provide valuable insights and help you manage your emotions more effectively.

Implementing Self-Care Practices

There are countless ways to practice self-care, and what works best will depend on your individual needs and preferences. Here are a few ideas to get you started:
- Physical self-care: This could involve regular exercise, eating a balanced diet, getting enough sleep, or taking

care of your physical appearance. These activities can help you feel good physically, which can in turn boost your mood and energy levels.

- Emotional self-care: This could involve activities that help you relax and de-stress, such as reading a book, listening to music, meditating, or taking a bath. It also involves acknowledging and expressing your emotions rather than suppressing them.
- Social self-care: This involves spending time with people who make you feel good about yourself, who support and understand you. This could be friends, family, or supportive communities.
- Intellectual self-care: This involves activities that stimulate your mind, such as reading, learning something new, solving puzzles, or engaging in creative pursuits.

Managing Reactions and Expectations

An integral part of dealing with toxic people is managing your reactions and expectations. Toxic people can often provoke strong emotional reactions, leading to stress and emotional turmoil. This is where mindfulness and self-care come into play.

With mindfulness, you learn to observe your emotions without judgment. Instead of getting caught up in the intensity of your feelings, you learn to take a step back, observe them, and let them pass without reacting impulsively. This ability to manage your reactions can be especially beneficial during interactions with toxic people.

Similarly, self-care helps in managing expectations. By taking care of your mental and emotional health, you can keep a realistic perspective on what to expect from your interactions with toxic individuals. It can help you realize that their behavior is a reflection of them, not you.

Setting Healthy Boundaries

Mindfulness and self-care also play a significant role in setting healthy boundaries. Mindfulness increases self-awareness, enabling you to recognize when your boundaries are being violated. Self-care, on the other hand, emphasizes the importance of prioritizing your well-being, which includes enforcing your boundaries.

Establishing boundaries is an important act of self-care. It involves asserting your needs and ensuring they are respected. This can be particularly challenging when dealing with toxic people, but it is a vital step in maintaining your emotional health.

Conclusion

Practicing mindfulness and self-care is an essential part of dealing with toxic people. They not only help you manage your reactions and expectations but also empower you to set and enforce healthy boundaries.

Mindfulness and self-care are not just strategies to be used in the face of toxicity; they are lifestyle changes that can improve your overall quality of life. By integrating them into your daily routine, you not only equip yourself to deal with toxic people more effectively but also enhance your well-being, resilience, and self-esteem.

We have now covered the importance of mindfulness and self-care in dealing with toxic people. As we progress through the next steps, we will continue to build upon the foundation laid so far, gradually equipping you with the tools and strategies needed to effectively navigate your interactions with toxic individuals.

6 CULTIVATING POSITIVE RELATIONSHIPS

An essential part of dealing with toxic people is understanding the value of positive relationships and interactions. When your energy is constantly being drained by toxicity, it is important to balance it with positivity. Positive relationships are those that bring joy, support, mutual respect, and beneficial exchange into your life. These interactions can serve as a counterbalance to the negative impacts of toxic relationships.

The Value of Positive Relationships

Positive relationships are those that foster growth, respect, and mutual understanding. They are characterized by a fair exchange of emotional support and a shared commitment to each other's well-being. This balance can be disrupted in toxic relationships, where one person's needs, desires, or emotions dominate the interaction.

In contrast, positive relationships are energizing, not draining. They provide a safe space for you to express your thoughts and feelings without fear of judgment or ridicule. They remind you of your worth, boost your confidence, and inspire you to pursue your goals and aspirations.

Moreover, positive relationships can provide a stark contrast to the negativity of toxic relationships, highlighting the difference between healthy and unhealthy interactions. This understanding can guide you in setting boundaries, recognizing red flags, and making informed decisions about who you allow into your life.

Positive Interactions: A Daily Practice

Positive interactions are not just about relationships; they are also about everyday encounters. A friendly exchange with a neighbor, a pleasant chat with a shopkeeper, or a warm greeting from a colleague can bring a moment of joy and positivity into your day.

Creating positive interactions can be as simple as offering a genuine compliment, expressing gratitude, or just being kind and considerate in your communications. Such practices not only bring positivity into your own life, but they also contribute to a more positive, supportive environment around you.

These initial discussions lay the foundation for understanding the importance of positive relationships and interactions when dealing with toxic individuals. Remember, cultivating positive relationships and interactions is a proactive step towards creating a healthy, supportive environment that can act as a buffer against the impacts of toxic relationships.

Practical Strategies for Generating Positive Relationships

Nurturing positive relationships involves more than just surrounding yourself with positive people; it also requires effort and commitment on your part. Here are a few strategies that can help:

Communication: Clear and respectful communication is the cornerstone of any healthy relationship. It involves expressing your thoughts and feelings honestly while also listening and being open to the other person's perspective.

Empathy: Understanding and sharing the feelings of others can foster a deeper emotional connection. Empathy involves acknowledging the other person's feelings without judgment, which can create an environment of trust and mutual respect.

Support: Offering support in times of need can strengthen your bonds with others. Whether it is emotional support, such as offering a listening ear, or practical support, like helping with a task, your efforts can help support a positive relationship.

Quality Time: Spending quality time together is another way to strengthen your relationships. This could involve shared hobbies, meaningful conversations, or simply enjoying each other's company. Such moments can create shared memories and deepen your emotional connection.

Creating Positive Interactions in Daily Life

Promoting positive interactions in daily life is a powerful way to counteract the effects of toxic relationships. Here are a few ways to create positive interactions:

Kindness: Small acts of kindness can make a big difference. Whether it is holding the door open for someone, offering a compliment, or helping a colleague, these acts can spread positivity.

Positivity: Adopting a positive attitude can influence your interactions. Instead of focusing on the negatives, try to find the silver lining in any situation.

Gratitude: Expressing gratitude can foster positivity. Whether it is appreciating a beautiful sunrise, being thankful for a supportive friend, or acknowledging a job well done, gratitude can turn ordinary moments into positive interactions.

Cultivating positive relationships and interactions can serve as a buffer against the negative effects of toxic people. The positivity you garner from these relationships and interactions can help bolster your resilience, making it easier to deal with toxic individuals when you encounter them.

The Impact of Positive Relationships and Interactions on Emotional Health

Positive relationships and interactions have a profound impact on emotional health. They serve as a source of joy, support, and encouragement, fostering a sense of belonging and enhancing self-esteem. They also provide a safety net of sorts, offering comfort and reassurance during difficult times.

Positive interactions, even those that seem insignificant, can contribute to a sense of community and belonging. They can make you feel valued and appreciated, boosting your mood and confidence. Over time, these interactions can help grow a positive outlook, making it easier to manage stress and adversity.

Moreover, positive relationships and interactions provide a healthy contrast to the negativity and stress often associated with toxic individuals. They remind you of what healthy, respectful interactions look like, helping you set expectations for your relationships.

Maintaining Positivity: A Lifelong Journey

Enriching positive relationships and interactions is a lifelong journey, one that requires time, effort, and patience. It is about making conscious choices about who you surround yourself with and how you engage with others.

Remember, you have the power to shape your social environment. By choosing to cultivate positive relationships and create positive interactions, you are taking a proactive step toward enhancing your well-being and resilience.

So, take a moment to reflect on the relationships in your life. Are they uplifting and supportive? Do they respect your boundaries? Do they foster growth and understanding? Similarly, consider your daily interactions. Do they bring joy and positivity into your life? If not, what steps can you take to change that?

In conclusion, focusing on positive relationships and interactions is a critical aspect of dealing with toxic people. It is about creating a supportive, positive environment that can buffer against the negativity of toxic relationships. It is about choosing to focus on positivity, even in the face of adversity.

7 SEEKING PROFESSIONAL HELP

In dealing with toxic people, it is crucial to recognize when professional help might be necessary. There can be situations where the impact of the toxic relationship significantly affects your mental health, and it may be too challenging to handle on your own.

Recognizing the Need for Professional Help

There are signs that might indicate the necessity for professional help. If you constantly feel stressed, anxious, or depressed due to the toxic relationship, or if you are having trouble sleeping, concentrating, or enjoying life as you used to, it may be time to seek advice from a professional.

Also, if you notice that your self-esteem is decreasing or you are starting to believe the negative things the toxic person is saying about you, a professional can provide you with strategies to counteract these harmful effects. A therapist or counselor can help you learn techniques to maintain your self-esteem and emotional well-being in the face of the negativity imposed by the toxic individual.

Remember, reaching out for professional help is not a sign of weakness but rather a strong, self-affirming act. It shows that you value your mental health and are ready to take steps to protect and improve it.

Exploring Different Forms of Professional Help

There is a variety of professional help available when dealing with toxic people and the stress they cause. Clinical psychologists and licensed therapists are trained to help you navigate emotional difficulties and improve your mental health.

Furthermore, life coaches can provide valuable guidance on managing difficult relationships and improving self-esteem. They can equip you with practical strategies for setting boundaries and dealing with toxic behavior.

Support groups are another useful resource. These are groups of people who are also dealing with toxic relationships. They provide a space to share experiences, learn from each other, and offer mutual support. This could be particularly helpful if you feel isolated or misunderstood in your experiences with the toxic person.

Understanding the Role of Therapy

Therapy, or counseling, plays a vital role in dealing with the emotional toll of toxic relationships. A licensed therapist can offer a safe, non-judgmental space for you to express your feelings and concerns. They can provide strategies to manage stress, rebuild self-esteem, and improve emotional well-being.

Therapists employ various techniques and therapeutic approaches to help you understand and navigate your emotions. Cognitive Behavioral Therapy (CBT), for instance, can help you identify and change negative thought patterns that may have been influenced by the toxic person. Similarly, trauma-focused therapy can be beneficial if the toxic relationship has resulted in traumatic experiences.

Moreover, therapists can provide guidance on setting boundaries and handling confrontations with the toxic person, skills that are essential in protecting yourself from further harm. They can help you devise a personalized coping strategy that suits your situation and meets your emotional needs.

Coaching and Its Benefits

Life coaching is another valuable resource that can assist you in dealing with toxic individuals. A life coach works with you to identify your goals and challenges and develop a plan to overcome them.

Coaches can offer practical strategies for managing difficult situations and people. They can help you enhance your communication skills, assertiveness, and confidence, all of which can empower you to stand up to toxic behavior.

In the context of toxic relationships, a life coach can assist in building resilience, nurturing self-esteem, and cultivating positivity in your life. They can provide tools and techniques to handle stress and negativity more effectively and create a life that aligns with your values and aspirations.

The Power of Support Groups

Support groups are a beneficial resource in managing the aftermath of toxic relationships. They consist of individuals who share similar experiences, creating a sense of community and mutual understanding that can be comforting.

In a support group, you can share your struggles, fears, and triumphs without judgment. Hearing others' stories can offer a different perspective on your situation and help you feel less alone in your experiences. It can also be a source of practical advice and coping strategies.

Furthermore, support groups can help you rebuild your social skills and confidence. By interacting with others in a respectful and supportive environment, you can regain trust in social relationships, which might have been eroded by the toxic person.

Accessing Professional Help and Making the Most Out of It

Professional help can be accessed in several ways. You can find therapists, counselors, and life coaches through healthcare providers, local community centers, or online platforms that connect clients with professionals. Support groups can also be found in community centers or online forums.

When seeking professional help, it is essential to ensure that the professional is licensed and experienced in dealing with toxic relationships or the specific issues you are facing. Feel free to ask about their qualifications, experience, and therapeutic approach before making a decision.

To make the most out of professional help, open communication is key. Be honest about your feelings, experiences, and goals. Remember, it is a collaborative process – your input and active participation are vital for the therapy or coaching to be effective.

Also, be patient with yourself. Healing and recovery take time. Each small step you take with the help of a professional is a victory and brings you closer to regaining control over your life and emotional well-being.

Virtual Support in the Digital Age

In the age of technology, virtual support has become an increasingly viable option for those seeking professional help. Online platforms provide access to therapists, counselors, and life coaches, removing geographical barriers and making help accessible right from the comfort of your home.

Online therapy platforms usually operate via video calls, allowing you to have face-to-face conversations with professionals. This can be especially beneficial if you have a busy schedule or live in an area with limited resources.

Similarly, there are numerous online support groups, forums, and communities for people dealing with toxic relationships. These platforms offer a space to share experiences, seek advice, and receive encouragement from individuals worldwide who are going through similar experiences.

The Role of Self-Help Resources

While professional help is crucial, self-help resources can also provide valuable guidance. Books, podcasts, blogs, and online courses offer a wealth of information on dealing with toxic people and the emotional turmoil they cause.

Many renowned psychologists, therapists, and coaches share their knowledge through these platforms. They provide practical advice, strategies, and insights that you can incorporate into your daily life. These resources can complement professional help, allowing you to continue learning and growing outside therapy or coaching sessions.

Remember, however, that self-help resources should not replace professional help, especially if you are dealing with severe emotional distress. They are tools to aid your understanding and help you navigate your situation more effectively.

Seeking professional help when needed is not merely about managing toxic relationships. It is a commitment to your mental health and personal growth. The journey might be challenging, but with the right help and resources, you are more than capable of overcoming the obstacles and nurturing healthier relationships. This concludes Step 7, where we emphasized the importance of seeking professional assistance and explored the different forms it can take, including traditional face-to-face therapy, online counseling, support groups, and self-help resources.

In the end, this type of support is another tool in your toolbox to help when dealing with toxic people and can be an empowering step. It provides you with the necessary support and equipment to protect your mental health, build resilience, and cultivate healthier relationships.

8 EMOTIONAL INTELLIGENCE

Understanding Emotional Intelligence

Emotional intelligence is the ability to understand, use, and manage your own emotions in positive ways to relieve stress, communicate effectively, empathize with others, overcome challenges, and defuse conflict. As such, it is a crucial skill when dealing with toxic individuals.

Being emotionally intelligent does not mean you ignore your emotions. On the contrary, it is about acknowledging them, understanding their origins, and managing how you react to them. In a situation involving a toxic person, emotional intelligence allows you to maintain control, minimizing the influence that person has over your emotional state.

Developing Emotional Self-Awareness

A key aspect of emotional intelligence is emotional self-awareness, the ability to recognize your emotions as they occur and understand the effect they can have on your thoughts and actions.

Increasing self-awareness starts with regular self-reflection. Paying attention to your emotional reactions and examining why you feel a certain way in response to specific interactions or situations can help you identify patterns and triggers.

By understanding your emotional responses better, you can start to manage them more effectively. You can recognize when a toxic person's behavior triggers an emotional response and take steps to control that response rather than allowing it to control you.

Improving Emotional Regulation

Emotional regulation refers to the process of influencing when and how you experience and express emotions. It involves strategies like cognitive reappraisal (changing how you think about a situation to change how you feel about it) and emotional suppression (inhibiting emotional expressions).

Building better emotional regulation skills allows you to control your reactions to a toxic person's behavior. Instead of letting their negativity provoke you into an emotional reaction, you can choose how to respond. This might mean taking a few moments to calm down, reconsidering the situation, or responding in a way that defuses potential conflict.

Enhancing Empathy

Empathy is a fundamental aspect of emotional intelligence. It refers to the ability to understand and share the feelings of others, which is vital in navigating social interactions and relationships. While it may seem counterintuitive to empathize with a toxic person, developing this skill can be incredibly helpful in managing your interactions with them.

When you empathize with someone, you try to see things from their perspective. This does not mean you justify their behavior, but understanding their motivations can provide you with valuable insight. It can help you discern patterns in their behavior, predict how they might react in certain situations, and devise more effective strategies for dealing with them.

To enhance your empathy, practice active listening. This involves not only hearing the words another person is saying but also understanding the emotions behind them. You might also try to imagine how you would feel in their position. Over time, these practices can help you become more in tune with other people's feelings and perspectives.

Developing Social Skills

The final component of emotional intelligence we will discuss is social skills. These are the skills we use to interact and communicate effectively with others. They include verbal and non-verbal communication, active listening, and the ability to maintain relationships.

Good social skills can help you keep interactions with toxic individuals from escalating into conflict. They can help you assert your boundaries more effectively, express your feelings and needs without provoking hostility, and maintain control of the conversation.

Improving social skills can be achieved through practice and reflection. Seek feedback from trusted friends or a mentor, observe others whom you think communicate effectively, and be open to learning from each social interaction. As your social skills improve, you will likely find that dealing with toxic people becomes more manageable.

Applying Emotional Intelligence in Interactions with Toxic Individuals

Developing emotional intelligence equips you with the skills needed to handle interactions with toxic individuals more effectively. Understanding your emotions enables you to maintain control, empathy helps you predict and understand their behavior, and good social skills allow you to communicate assertively and respectfully.

With these tools at your disposal, you can navigate the challenges posed by toxic people without compromising your own well-being. Remember, the goal is not to change them but to change how you respond to them.

A Vital Part of Emotional Intelligence

As you develop emotional intelligence, it is essential to emphasize self-care. Remember, managing your interactions with toxic people can be draining, both emotionally and mentally. Regularly taking time to rest, relax, and rejuvenate is crucial.

Consider activities that help you relieve stress, such as exercise, meditation, or spending time with loved ones. These activities not only help you unwind but also improve your ability to regulate your emotions.

A Practical Application of Emotional Intelligence

In Step 3 we discussed the importance of setting boundaries. Setting boundaries is an essential skill when dealing with toxic people. By defining what behavior you will and will not accept, you can protect yourself from the negative impact of a toxic person's behavior.

Having good emotional intelligence can make setting boundaries easier. If you are aware of your emotions and can regulate them effectively, you are more likely to recognize when a line has been crossed. And with strong social skills, you can assert these boundaries respectfully and confidently.

Recognizing When Help is Needed

Emotional intelligence also involves recognizing when you need help and seeking it. Dealing with toxic people can sometimes lead to situations that are difficult to handle alone.

If you find that a toxic person in your life is causing you significant distress or if your efforts to manage the situation are not working, it might be time to seek professional help. A mental health professional can provide strategies and tools for dealing with toxic individuals and can offer a supportive environment to discuss your feelings and concerns.

In conclusion, cultivating emotional intelligence is a powerful approach to dealing with toxic people. It allows you to understand and manage your emotions, empathize with others, and enhance your social skills, empowering you to navigate difficult relationships more effectively. Take your time to develop these skills, be patient with yourself, and remember the importance of self-care. Your journey towards dealing with toxic individuals more effectively is a marathon, not a sprint, and every step you take towards improving your emotional intelligence is a step in the right direction.

9 DEALING WITH TOXIC INDIVIDUALS

As we move into practical strategies for interacting with toxic people, it is important to remember that the approach will often depend on the context. Certain techniques may be more applicable to the workplace, within the family, or in social settings. However, regardless of the context, a few general strategies can be beneficial across the board.

High-Level Overview of Strategies

One universal strategy is maintaining strong personal boundaries. Toxic individuals often disregard the personal space, feelings, or rights of others. By establishing and communicating your boundaries clearly, you can protect yourself from their negative impact.

Another critical strategy is mastering the art of non-reactivity. Toxic individuals often behave provocatively to elicit reactions from others. By learning to remain calm and not engaging with their negativity, you can avoid being pulled into unnecessary conflicts.

Lastly, do not hesitate to seek professional help if dealing with toxic people becomes overwhelming. A mental health professional can provide additional tools and strategies tailored to your specific situation.

Now let us delve into some strategies suited to different contexts, starting with the workplace.

Navigating Toxicity in the Workplace

Work environments can often harbor toxic individuals due to the competitive and high-pressure nature of many industries. A crucial strategy in such contexts is assertive communication. You should clearly express your boundaries and feelings when they are crossed. Use "I" statements to avoid sounding confrontational - for example, "I feel overlooked when you dismiss my ideas during meetings."

Also, consider leveraging HR or management in extreme cases. They can provide mediation or take more direct action if a colleague's behavior is severely impacting your productivity or well-being.

Addressing Toxicity within the Family

Family situations can prove particularly challenging when dealing with toxicity due to the deeper emotional connections and complex dynamics at play. When dealing with toxic family members, it is essential to maintain healthy emotional distance. This does not necessarily mean reducing contact (though, in some cases, it might), but rather not letting their negative behaviors affect your emotional state.

Another useful strategy within family settings is to use family gatherings or meetings as a platform to express your concerns. This can be done individually or with the support of family members who understand and acknowledge the problem. Using this kind of collective approach can often lead to more constructive outcomes.

Family therapy is another potent tool for dealing with toxic family members. With a skilled therapist, families can uncover underlying issues, improve communication, and work towards a healthier family dynamic.

Handling Toxicity in Social Settings

In social settings, toxic individuals can put a dampener on gatherings and events. One effective strategy here is to limit your interaction with such individuals. Try not to engage them in deep or meaningful conversations which they could potentially twist and manipulate.

Utilizing assertive communication, as mentioned in the workplace context, is again important here. If you are uncomfortable with someone's behavior, it is entirely within your rights to let them know.

Finally, remember that you can choose your social circle. If a friend consistently displays toxic behavior, it might be time to reconsider whether you want to maintain that friendship. While ending a friendship is never easy, it is important to surround yourself with people who respect and support you.

The strategies outlined here provide a framework for dealing with toxic individuals in various contexts. By adapting these strategies to your specific situations, you can protect your mental and emotional well-being and navigate challenging relationships more effectively.

Conflict Resolution Techniques with Toxic Individuals

Conflict resolution is an invaluable skill when interacting with toxic individuals. The ability to manage and resolve conflicts without losing your integrity and peace of mind can significantly reduce the impact of toxic individuals on your life.

1. **Active Listening:** This involves truly hearing and understanding the other person's perspective, even if you don't agree with it. By showing that you are listening, you can often de-escalate conflicts and make the other person more open to hearing your perspective.
2. **Use "I" Statements:** As previously mentioned, using "I" statements can help prevent the other person from feeling attacked. For instance, instead of saying, "You never listen to me," try saying, "I feel unheard when I share my ideas."
3. **Avoid Escalation:** Toxic individuals often thrive on drama and conflict. By refusing to engage in heated

arguments and maintaining a calm, measured demeanor, you can prevent conflicts from escalating.

4. **Seek Neutral Ground:** If you are engaged in a conflict with a toxic person, try to move the conversation to a neutral topic or seek common ground. This can help defuse tension and potentially shift the interaction to a more positive trajectory.

5. **Use Mediation if Needed:** In more serious conflicts, consider seeking a mediator. This could be a mutual friend, a family member, a supervisor at work, or even a professional mediator or counselor.

Remember, dealing with toxic individuals can be draining and challenging. However, with these strategies and techniques, you can protect your mental health and navigate these challenging relationships more effectively. Each situation is unique, and it might require some adjustments to these strategies, but staying patient and committed to maintaining your well-being is the key.

Conflict Resolution Techniques in Different Settings

Let us consider applying the above strategies within the three contexts: the workplace, family, and social settings. The application of these strategies varies slightly depending on the context and the relationships involved.

At work, assertive communication, active listening, and seeking neutral ground are particularly useful. For example, in team meetings, active listening can facilitate more productive discussions. Additionally, if you find yourself in a heated debate, steering the conversation towards a neutral or work-related topic can help defuse tension.

In more severe cases, it might be necessary to involve human resources or a manager to mediate the conflict, as mentioned above. Remember, it is their role to ensure a healthy, productive work environment for all employees.

Within the family, mediation can be especially useful, given the complex dynamics and long-standing relationships. This could involve a respected family member or a professional mediator or therapist. Family therapy, as mentioned earlier, can be a potent tool for resolving conflicts and improving overall family dynamics.

Assertive communication is also crucial in family settings. Letting family members know when their behavior is hurtful or unacceptable while ensuring you respect their feelings and perspectives can lead to more understanding and less conflict.

In social settings, you have more control over whom you interact with and how much. Limiting interactions with toxic individuals and avoiding engaging them in deep or contentious discussions can help prevent conflicts. Active listening and assertive communication can also be beneficial in these settings, helping you manage interactions without escalating conflicts.

Keep in mind, dealing with conflicts requires patience and practice. The more you apply these techniques, the more naturally they will come to you and the better equipped you will be to manage conflicts with toxic individuals across various settings. Remember, maintaining your mental health and well-being should always be your priority.

Seeking External Help and Support

As discussed previously, an often overlooked yet crucial aspect of dealing with toxic individuals and resolving conflicts is seeking external help and support. This does not necessarily mean professional help, although therapists and counselors can provide invaluable guidance as we discussed previously.

Friends, mentors, and supportive individuals in your life can act as a sounding board, allowing you to vent, seek advice, and gain a different perspective on your situation. These individuals can provide comfort, practical advice, and sometimes even intervene directly if the situation calls for it.

Implementing Personal Boundaries

An essential, and hopefully not new by now, strategy in dealing with toxic individuals is establishing and enforcing personal boundaries. These boundaries safeguard your emotional and mental well-being, help you maintain your self-esteem, and allow you to disengage from situations that are harmful or emotionally draining.

Boundaries could be related to time (for example, deciding not to engage with a toxic colleague outside of work hours), emotional investment (choosing not to get emotionally involved in a toxic person's dramas), or personal values (standing firm on your beliefs and not allowing a toxic individual to make you compromise them).

Establishing boundaries often means saying 'no' to people and situations that are harmful to you. It is crucial to remember that saying 'no' is not a sign of weakness or rudeness. It is a way of taking care of your emotional health and asserting your self-worth.

The Role of Forgiveness

While it may seem counterintuitive, forgiveness is an effective strategy for dealing with toxic individuals. This does not mean forgetting or excusing their behavior. Instead, it is about letting go of your anger and resentment towards them. This is not for their benefit but for yours. Holding onto negative emotions can be damaging to your mental health, and it gives the toxic person more power over your emotions.

Forgiving a toxic person involves accepting that you cannot change them, only your reaction to them. It also means understanding that their toxicity is their issue, not yours.

By combining these strategies and techniques, you can better navigate interactions with toxic individuals in various settings, maintain your peace of mind, and protect your emotional and mental health. Remember, every situation is unique and might require an adaptation of these strategies, but the central focus should always be your well-being.

The Power of Perspective

Perspective plays a critical role when dealing with toxic individuals. Shifting your mindset and the way you perceive their behavior can profoundly affect how you respond to them. By recognizing that their toxic behavior is a reflection of their internal struggles, you can detach your self-worth and emotional state from their actions.

Viewing a toxic person's actions as a result of their issues rather than a direct attack on you can help reduce the impact of their toxicity. It is not about excusing their behavior but rather about protecting your emotional health by reframing the situation.

Practicing Self-Care

Amidst dealing with toxicity and conflict, never underestimate the importance of self-care. This includes engaging in activities that you enjoy and that help you relax and recharge. It can be as simple as taking a warm bath, going for a walk, reading a book, or spending time with loved ones.

Regularly practicing mindfulness and relaxation techniques such as meditation, yoga, or deep breathing exercises can help manage stress and anxiety associated with toxic individuals. Keeping a journal can also be beneficial, providing an outlet for your feelings and helping you gain insight into your emotions and reactions.

Acceptance and Letting Go

Acceptance does not mean tolerating toxic behavior or allowing it to continue unchecked. Rather, it is about acknowledging that you cannot control or change the behavior of a toxic person, but you can control your reactions to them. It involves understanding that some people may not change, no matter how much effort you put into trying to help or change them.

Letting go is the next step after acceptance. This could mean cutting ties with the toxic person, reducing your interactions with them, or simply letting go of the emotional impact they have on you. It is a challenging process, but it is crucial for your emotional health and well-being.

Conclusion

In conclusion, dealing with toxic individuals and managing conflicts with them is a complex process, requiring a variety of strategies and techniques. From understanding the characteristics of toxic people, developing emotional intelligence, and assertive communication, to conflict resolution techniques and establishing personal boundaries, each step is a part of your arsenal to protect your mental health and maintain your peace of mind.

Remember, it is essential to prioritize your emotional and mental well-being above all else. With these strategies, you are not just surviving in a world with toxic individuals but thriving.

10 GROWING FROM EXPERIENCE

Adversity, in all its forms, presents an opportunity for growth. Encountering and dealing with toxic people is no exception. Though it may be challenging, this adversity can become a catalyst for significant personal development and emotional maturation. When you survive an encounter with a toxic individual or successfully navigate a conflict, you develop resilience. This resilience is not just the ability to bounce back from a difficult experience but also encompasses the capacity to grow and adapt as a result of the encounter.

Developing resilience involves consciously cultivating positive habits and attitudes, such as optimism, understanding, and managing emotions, maintaining a supportive social network, and seeing challenges as opportunities rather than insurmountable problems. It is about recognizing that you have the ability to control your response to a situation, regardless of how tough it is.

Turning Adversity into Strength

Your interactions with toxic individuals provide an opportunity to learn more about your personal boundaries, emotional triggers, and conflict resolution abilities. Each conflict, each difficult conversation, and each moment of emotional discomfort is a chance to understand yourself better. You become more attuned to your needs and emotions and, in turn, better equipped to manage similar situations in the future.

This process of self-discovery can lead to increased emotional intelligence. Emotional intelligence is not only about understanding your emotions but also about being empathetic toward others' feelings. In the context of dealing with toxic people, this heightened emotional intelligence will allow you to navigate interactions with grace, understanding, and firmness.

Understanding When to Move On

Recognizing when to cut ties and move away from a toxic relationship is a critical aspect of dealing with toxic people. It is essential to understand that not all relationships can or should be saved. Some relationships, especially those with toxic individuals, can be more harmful than beneficial.

The decision to walk away from a toxic relationship is a difficult one, fraught with emotional turmoil. However, it is vital to prioritize your mental and emotional health. Signs that it may be time to move away include feeling consistently drained or unhappy after interactions, noticing that the relationship is impacting your other relationships negatively, and experiencing a significant dip in your self-esteem or mental health.

The act of moving on from a toxic relationship is not about spite or revenge but about self-care. It is a demonstration of respect and love for oneself. It is also a choice that often leads to growth, as it requires a deep understanding of personal boundaries and self-worth.

Embracing Self-Care

Self-care has been talk about countless times during these ten steps, and is vital when moving away from a toxic relationship. It means taking the time to heal, reflect, and regain your strength. This may involve seeking professional help such as counseling or therapy. Therapists can provide strategies for handling the emotional turmoil that often accompanies the end of a toxic relationship.

Self-care also encompasses maintaining physical health. Regular exercise, a healthy diet, and sufficient sleep all contribute to emotional well-being. Taking care of your physical health can help mitigate the physical symptoms of stress and provide a sense of control in a tumultuous time.

Remember, self-care is not selfish. It is a necessary component of emotional health. By taking care of your needs, you ensure that you are in a better position to take care of others' needs and handle future conflicts more effectively.

Finding Support

In times of emotional turmoil, it is important to lean on your support network. Friends, family, and loved ones can provide much-needed comfort and advice. If you are comfortable, share your experiences with them. Often, simply speaking about your experiences can provide relief and perspective.

Forgiveness and Letting Go

Forgiveness is an integral part of moving on from a toxic relationship. It does not mean forgetting what happened or absolving the other person of their wrongs. Instead, forgiveness is about releasing resentment and anger that could hold you back from healing and moving forward.

Forgiveness takes time and is not always easy. It is a personal process that happens on your own timeline. It is okay if you are not ready to forgive right away. What is important is to be open to the idea of forgiveness and to work towards it as part of your healing process.

Letting go does not mean ignoring the past or suppressing your emotions. Instead, it involves accepting your experiences, learning from them, and then releasing them so they no longer hold power over you. Letting go allows you to focus on the present and the future, which is especially important when trying to move on from a toxic relationship.

Turning a New Leaf

Emerging from a toxic relationship or encounter can feel like a rebirth. It presents an opportunity to reevaluate what you want from your relationships and how you want to be treated. Use this opportunity to establish healthier patterns in your relationships and to assert your boundaries more effectively. Remember, you are not alone in this journey. Reach out for help when you need it and be patient with yourself. Every step you take is a step towards a healthier, happier you.

When moving on, consider what boundaries were crossed in the toxic relationship. What made you uncomfortable? What actions or words hurt you? Once you have identified these, you can establish clear boundaries in your future relationships to avoid repeating past patterns.

Assertiveness is crucial in setting your own limits. It is about expressing your needs in a respectful and firm manner. It takes practice, especially if you are not used to it. However, the payoff is worth it. Doing this not only protects you but also fosters mutual respect in your relationships.

Becoming Self-Reliant

Having dealt with a toxic person, you might find that your self-esteem and self-reliance have been undermined. This is why it is critical to rebuild your self-reliance when moving on.

Building self-reliance involves trusting in your abilities and judgments. It is about knowing that you are capable of taking care of yourself and making the right decisions for your life. To foster self-reliance, take small steps to challenge yourself. This could be anything from taking on a new responsibility at work to traveling solo. Over time, these small victories will boost your confidence and self-reliance.

Seeking Positivity

After experiencing a toxic relationship, it is essential to seek out positivity. Surround yourself with positive influences, engage in activities you love, and practice positive self-talk.

Positivity is not about ignoring the negative aspects of life. It is about focusing on the good without overlooking the bad. It is acknowledging your pain and struggles while also appreciating your strengths and victories. The goal is to cultivate a balanced, optimistic perspective that can help you navigate future challenges.

Embracing Change

Finally, moving on from a toxic relationship involves embracing change. It is accepting that things will be different, and that is okay. It is allowing yourself to change as a result of your experiences.

Embracing change is not always easy. It can be scary and uncertain. However, change is also an opportunity for growth and improvement. It allows you to break away from harmful patterns and develop healthier ones.

Remember, you have survived a toxic relationship and emerged stronger. You have the strength to adapt to change and to create a life that brings you happiness and fulfillment. This experience, as challenging as it was, has given you a deeper understanding of yourself and your resilience. Embrace this newfound understanding and let it guide you as you move forward.

Toxic relationships are challenging and can leave lasting scars. However, they also present opportunities for personal growth. By utilizing these strategies and keeping your well-being in focus, you can turn a negative experience into a stepping stone toward a happier, healthier future.

Diving Deeper into Forgiveness

While often challenging, forgiveness can be a powerful part of the healing process and personal growth. Forgiving does not mean forgetting what happened or justifying the toxic person's behavior. It simply means releasing the anger and resentment you have been holding onto and allowing yourself to heal from the emotional wounds inflicted.

The act of forgiveness is more about you than the person who hurt you. It is about freeing yourself from the burden of bitterness and giving yourself permission to move forward. Practicing forgiveness can be as simple as writing a letter to the person you are forgiving (without the necessity of sending it) or just deciding in your heart to let go of the pain.

It is worth noting that forgiveness is a personal decision and a process. It takes time, and it is okay if you are not ready yet. But when you do reach that point, you will find that it brings a great deal of relief and opens the door to emotional healing.

Cultivating Self-Compassion

Growing from the experience of a toxic relationship also involves cultivating self-compassion. You might have been hard on yourself, blaming yourself for what happened. It is crucial to understand that it was not your fault. Toxic people are responsible for their actions, not you.

Self-compassion is about treating yourself with the same kindness and understanding you would show a close friend. It involves acknowledging your own feelings and allowing yourself to be imperfect. Practice self-compassion by recognizing when you are being harsh on yourself and replacing negative self-talk with positive affirmations.

Personal Development and Growth

Every experience, even the negative ones, offers valuable lessons for personal growth. Toxic relationships often provide hard yet significant lessons about self-worth, boundaries, and emotional resilience.

Reflect on what you have learned about yourself from this experience. Maybe you have discovered new personal strengths or identified areas for improvement. Use these insights as a guide for personal development. You might choose to read self-help books, attend workshops, or seek counseling. The goal is to use the experience as a catalyst for positive change, to grow as a person, and to ensure healthier relationships in the future.

Conclusion

Remember, the goal of moving on is not to erase the past or pretend it did not happen. It is about learning from the experience, growing as a person, and moving forward with resilience and grace. With time and effort, you can turn adversity into strength and discover a newfound sense of self-worth, independence, and personal growth.

SUMMARY

Our journey began with an exploration of what constitutes toxicity in relationships. We learned that a toxic relationship can be any relationship in which one person is harmed, physically or emotionally, by the other. It is not restricted to romantic relationships but can occur in familial relations, friendships, and professional relationships. We emphasized the importance of recognizing toxic behaviors such as manipulation, constant criticism, belittling, and disregard for personal boundaries. Gaining the ability to identify toxic behaviors is the first step in dealing with toxic individuals.

Understanding Your Role and Setting Boundaries

As we moved forward, we delved into the roles we play in these toxic dynamics and how we might be unconsciously allowing toxicity to thrive. We highlighted the importance of introspection and understanding one's self-esteem, assertiveness, and patterns of behavior that might make one susceptible to staying in toxic relationships. Additionally, we stressed the importance of setting healthy boundaries. By doing so, we assert our needs and desires, promoting respect and mutual understanding, which are pillars of any healthy relationship.

Effective Communication and Emotional Intelligence

A crucial segment of our journey focused on enhancing our communication skills and emotional intelligence. It is often challenging to express our feelings and needs effectively, especially in a charged situation with a toxic individual. However, it is possible through patient practice and mindfulness. Coupled with an understanding of emotional intelligence, this skill equips us to handle confrontations better and navigate challenging conversations. It allows us to empathize with others, control our reactions, and foster healthier interactions.

Practical Strategies and Conflict Resolution

We then addressed practical strategies for dealing with toxic individuals in various contexts, be it at work, within the family, or in social settings. The importance of prioritizing one's mental and emotional health cannot be overstated. Techniques for managing and resolving conflicts without losing your own integrity and peace of mind were also explored. These strategies are practical, actionable, and aim to empower the reader in the face of adversity.

Personal Growth and Moving On

In the final stretch of our journey, we explored how to use these experiences as opportunities for personal growth and understanding, ultimately turning adversity into strength. Dealing with toxic people and navigating such relationships can be a learning experience that promotes resilience and personal development. Importantly, it can lead to heightened emotional intelligence, improved assertiveness, and better communication skills.

Additionally, we discussed the critical aspect of understanding when it is time to cut ties and move on from a toxic relationship. This decision is never easy, but it is sometimes the healthiest choice for one's well-being. Guidance on how to do so in a respectful and healthy way was provided, emphasizing the importance of self-care during this process.

Thriving Beyond Toxicity

Finally, we arrived at the end of our journey, emphasizing the possibility of thriving beyond toxicity and leading a healthier, happier life. Despite the challenges faced, remember that your worth is not determined by someone else's behavior. You have the strength and the resources to move beyond toxic situations and thrive.

Dealing with toxicity is a universal experience, but it is crucial to remember that everyone's journey is unique. There are countless paths to healing and thriving beyond toxicity. Each step in this book is meant to be a guide, a helping hand on your journey. Whether you are identifying toxic behavior for the first time or working on severing ties with a toxic person, each step is a victory in its own right.

Enduring Lessons and Tools for the Journey Ahead

One of the most enduring lessons from our journey is the importance of self-love and self-respect. This is more than a feel-good sentiment. It is a practical tool for navigating toxic relationships and situations. When you value yourself, you are less likely to accept poor treatment from others. You recognize that you deserve respect and kindness, and you are more willing to stand up for yourself when others attempt to undermine your worth.

Another significant lesson is the power of boundaries. Toxic individuals often disregard or disrespect others' boundaries, leading to stress, anxiety, and conflict. By asserting your boundaries and sticking to them, you can protect your well-being and prevent others from taking advantage of you.

The practice of mindfulness and emotional intelligence also emerged as powerful tools in dealing with toxic individuals. Being mindful of your emotions, thoughts, and reactions can help you manage challenging situations more effectively. It can also help you recognize and avoid the triggers that may lead to conflict with toxic individuals.

The Path Forward

Our journey has come full circle. From identifying toxic individuals, understanding their behavior, building emotional resilience, setting boundaries, adopting effective communication strategies, employing conflict resolution techniques to finally cutting ties and moving on - we have covered significant ground in our quest to thrive beyond toxicity.

Each step of this journey requires courage, patience, and perseverance. There will be setbacks and struggles, but remember that every step forward, no matter how small, is progress. Progress towards healthier relationships, towards a better understanding of yourself, towards a life that is not defined by toxicity but thrives in spite of it.

Reflections

Reflecting on our journey, it becomes evident how integral self-awareness is in navigating relationships, particularly those with toxic individuals. Self-awareness allows us to recognize unhealthy patterns and behavior, both in ourselves and in others. It is the first step towards making meaningful changes in how we interact with others and how we allow them to interact with us.

An interesting perspective that emerged during our journey is the understanding that toxicity does not exist in a vacuum. It is usually a reflection of deeper issues and insecurities harbored by the toxic person. This is not to excuse their behavior but rather to provide insight that can help us deal with them more effectively. Remember, their negativity is about them, not you.

In the course of dealing with toxic people, remember that it's not about winning every battle. Sometimes, it is about knowing when to walk away. Knowing when it is no longer worth the emotional cost. Remember, walking away is not a sign of defeat but an act of self-preservation and self-respect.

Lastly, we should not forget the incredible resilience and strength that resides within each of us. We are not defined by our encounters with toxic individuals but by how we rise above them. We are not victims but survivors and warriors. We have the ability to grow from these experiences and use them as stepping stones toward becoming stronger, wiser, and more compassionate individuals.

Closing

As we bring these ten steps to a close, let us remind ourselves that thriving beyond toxicity is not a destination but a continuous journey. An excursion towards healthier relationships, towards greater self-awareness, towards emotional well-being.

Despite the challenges and hardships, remember to appreciate the journey and the growth that comes with it. There is no such thing as a life entirely free of adversity. But it is in our power to turn adversity into strength. To use our experiences as the bridge that can lead us toward personal growth and understanding.

This is the essence of thriving beyond toxicity: transforming adversity into strength, learning from our experiences, and growing from them. May this book serve as a guide and a companion on your journey. May it empower you to navigate and overcome the toxicity in your life, and to emerge stronger, wiser, and more resilient.

Thank you for embarking on this journey with me. I hope you found the information and strategies useful, and that they will serve you well in your journey ahead.

Printed in Great Britain
by Amazon

24863294R00046